Poems fo
Shakesp

Poems for Shakespeare 10

Edited with an Introduction by Charles Osborne

Bishopsgate Press
Southwark 1987

The front cover illustration is by John Spring

The text illustrations by Rockwell Kent are reproduced by kind permission of Doubleday & Co. Inc.

Poems for Shakespeare.
   10.
   1. Shakespeare, William, in fiction, drama,
   poetry, etc. 2. English poetry – 20th
   century
   I. Osborne, Charles II. International
   Shakespeare Globe Centre
   821'.9140803   PR2935

   ISBN 1-85219-011-6

All enquiries and requests relevant to this title should be sent to the publisher, Bishopsgate Press Ltd., 37 Union Street, London SE1 1SE

Printed by Whitstable Litho Ltd., Whitstable, Kent.

Contents

INTRODUCTION   9

TED HUGHES
A FULL HOUSE   11

GEORGE MACBETH
THE HERALDS ASSOCIATE LADY MACBETH
  WITH KEITH DOUGLAS   25

GILES GORDON
HAMLET AND THE FIRST CLOWN (GRAVE-DIGGER):
  VARIOUS PROBLEMS UNRAVELLED   26

ANTHONY THWAITE
A READING OF DOCTOR SAMUEL JOHNSON'S
  NOTES ON THE PLAYS: 1765   30

PETER READING
POEM   31

MICHAEL SCHMIDT
ALL.HAPPINESSE.AND.THAT.ETERNITIE   32

ROY FULLER
SHAKESPEARE STUDIES   33

DANNIE ABSE
A CONSPICUOUS COUPLE   34

PETE MORGAN
GET THEE GLASS EYES: 36

DAVID HARSENT
THE ANALYSAND   38

JOHN COTTON
MATTHEW GOFFE   41

A. L. ROWSE
LINES FOR WILLIAM SHAKESPEARE 42

JOHN FULLER
DAUGHTER 44

ALAN BROWNJOHN
WAR – THOUGHTS 47

ROGER WODDIS
LEARNING FROM THE MASTER 49

D. J. ENRIGHT
NEW READINGS 50

PENELOPE SHUTTLE
THE HORSE WHO LOVES ME 52

DAVID SWEETMAN
FORTUNE AND MEN'S EYES 54

EDWIN MORGAN
THE BEAR 55

GAVIN EWART
THE ORACLE SPEAKS IN THE DRESSING ROOM
OF MR. PATRICK STEWART AT THE BARBICAN,
BEFORE A PERFORMANCE OF THE WINTER'S TALE 56

LAURENCE COTTERELL
DEEPMAN CAIUS KENT 58

PATRICIA BEER
NINNY'S TOMB 59

PETER REDGROVE
SISTER 60

CHARLES TOMLINSON
VARIATION 62

Illustrations

by Rockwell Kent

"O! how thy worth with manners
may I sing – " SONNETS   Frontispiece

                                          FACING PAGE

"Why is my lord enrag'd against
his love?" ANTONY AND CLEOPATRA   12

"Alas! poor Yorick." HAMLET   26

'Tis Troilus! there's a man!" TROILUS AND CRESSIDA   47

"He tells her something
That makes her blood look out" THE WINTER'S TALE   56

Introduction

This is the tenth volume of *Poems for Shakespeare*. These volumes have not quite been an annual event, for the first was published fifteen years ago; however, they have appeared in most years, and a majority of the leading poets of this country have contributed to them, as have a number of distinguished poets from abroad. As this year's editor, I decided to invite my favourite British poets to contribute, and to allow them a very free rein. Some editors of earlier volumes had asked for poems addressed to Shakespeare, or poems about Shakespeare, or poems developing a theme from one of the plays, or poems taking as their starting point a specific line from a Shakespeare play. I have gone back to the attitude adopted by Christopher Hampton, who edited the very first volume in 1972. Recognizing that there are many ways of honouring Shakespeare, he imposed no limitation upon his contributors, except that of length, allowing them to respond to the occasion as they thought fit.

All twenty-five of the poets I invited to contribute accepted the invitation, and in the event only one of them failed to deliver: I had expected two or three more to fall by the wayside, for one cannot always be certain of producing a poem simply by intending to do so. With the exception of the Poet Laureate, Ted Hughes, whose 'Full House' of thirteen poems opens this collection, all the poets were asked to write poems of no more than fifty lines, and surprisingly all but three managed to stay within that limit. The poems are immensely varied: in some the Shakespearian references are easier to follow than in others. But I hope the reader will find, as I do, that they make an enjoyable and impressive collection.

Charles Osborne

This whole project, of the poems and the rebuilding of The Globe Theatre, has been the brain child of the American actor, producer and director Sam Wanamaker.

TED HUGHES

A FULL HOUSE

1. Queen of Hearts

Venereal, uterine heat.
Smothering breast-fruit.
The poor boy gasped to be out.

Hell-mouth he could hear.
The many mouthed hound in there
Started his heart a hare.

Daddy jumped, the god of war,
From under her skirts, as a scythe-tusked boar.
Mortal frailty tore.

Willy's blood a shower
Of fertiliser for,
Where he fell, a flower.

2. Queen of Spades

The Serpent Of Old Nile
Coiled in a fig-tree
Queen Cleopatra's
Affable, familiar
Hypodermic smile.

Fruit of the tree he seized
And was darkly kissed.

And melted into air
Twenty years had gone
Dreaming of passion on
That bed in the East.

3. Queen of Clubs

Three Corbies in a tree
Sang to Macbeth
Maid, Wife, Mother
We are tragedy
Queen of Birth and Death
And there is no other.

Your Fate's a double coil.
For Will to grab the crown
Mother, Maid, Wife
You must kill your Soul
(We'll help you get it done)
And still hang on to your life.

Such soulful, wilful acts
The shadows of your limbs
Wife, Mother, Maid
Shall be history's facts . . .
The crown plucked in these dreams
Paid for by Cromwell's head.

14

4. Queen of Diamonds

My son told such a tale...
His father killed by an Owl!

Dressed for the funeral
He started to play the Fool.

Dreaming he'd married me
He cried: "It cannot be!"

His sanity took the veil
In Avon's darkest pool.

Succession in a pall
Crazed him to murder us all . . .

Pausing for no farewell
I fled into this pearl.

5. King Of Hearts

My Will shall be
What I have planned:
My treasure, my land
Split into three.

One third I pay
To help Anne's age
Put her youth's rage
And hate away.

To Judith one
For who will marry
Memento Mori
Of my son?

And for Sue
The final part
Includes my heart
That is pierced through

By my own Lance
In young Edmund's
Bastard Edmund's
Lineal hands.

Envoi

And to God, Her
   Of triple power
Locked with the hoodlum
   Of this hour.

6. King of Spades

Tarquin the King's
Besieging eye
Sacked Lucrece's
Chastity.

Which, it seems,
Wore such a crown
Kingship itself
Was tumbled down.

The bubble of State
We see from this
Balloons from lips
That were made to kiss.

7. King of Clubs

A cripple soon
Can find a fault.
Speak of my lameness
I straight will halt.

I carry a sack
Of limbless pain.
Body deposed
The mind will reign.

The nimble fools
Of human pride
Shall be the toys
Of what I hide.

8. King of Diamonds

The Cabalist is old.
Crucibles thrice thirteen
Alchemised air to gold,

His soul's incarnate stain,
The tigerish, upstart crow,
To a self of diamond stone.

Sword and Cup can go;
All trumpery that held
The invisible in awe.

Familiar, daemon child,
A howling banshee, rides
A rainbow from the world.

And as the pageant fades,
Warming his master's grave
The calloused Golem hides

Clutching the broken staff
Three fathoms under the prayer
And terminal, wild laugh

Of his great lord who prays
The sea-monster ashore
And feeds it with his plays.

9. Knave of Hearts

Hal moistens his lips.
  After many a try
At last he slips
  Through the needle's eye

To sew the tap–
  –estry of a new England.
But he's only the tip
  Of the glory-hole tangle

Old Adam packed in
  To the quaking sack
Of the fat Knight's skin . . .
  Will the thread break?

10. Knave of Spades

The Sulphur, Charcoal, Nitrate of his gunnery
Proportioned Othello.
Who fell for this fellow?
A blonde pure as a taper in a nunnery.

A light, light lass, a dark, heavy chap,
And a touch of evil laughter . . .
Boom, the whole lot goes up
Unhappily ever after.

11. Knave of Clubs

Nature's child
Looks at men's graves
As the sun
Watches the waves.

And as the wind
Does what it likes
Finds no bar
To his thoughts and looks.

Wherefore should he
Be other than
Death itself
To play at man?

For all it needs
To rule alone
Taking all
Is to love none.

12. Knave Of Diamonds

As Mary bore
The Son so mourned
Tortured, murdered
And returned

Timon gives all.
Hands close and take.
Open to render
Hatred back.

In X-ray blink
Baboons revealed
The skulls for which
Their lips had smiled.

He hurls the bomb
From his mother's womb
That blows the species
To kingdom come.

13. Joker

On all my stages
Not to be heard
On all my pages
Never a word

Where there is nobody
A soothing
Suffering all
Suffers nothing

GEORGE MACBETH

THE HERALDS ASSOCIATE LADY MACBETH WITH KEITH DOUGLAS

Returning over the nightmare ground
We found the three hundred bad days
Still unburied. The combatants
Were in separate countries, but

Flies crawled on their blood.
She had hit his heart
With one like the entry of the sense of death
And he was there

With her photograph
In his guts, overgrown with blue flowers
Beautiful as the AIDS virus, a body

In the sands of time. She would have cried
To see the poetry strewn around
Him, the fighting suit of an enemy
Who died for love. And the brain yawning
With nothing now, the eyes like mirrors for pain.

Only the little word forget-me-not
Like a font
In a ruined cathedral, was what
She might have washed her hands of it all in, the

Lady Macbeth of a haunted Egypt.

GILES GORDON

HAMLET AND THE FIRST CLOWN (GRAVE-DIGGER): VARIOUS PROBLEMS UNRAVELLED

The grave-digger got it wrong
but who could gainsay him?
His mate he had dispatched to Yaughan
for a stoup or two. Or four.

The skull was *not* Yorick's.
The grave-digger (wormwood, rotten wood)
confused the jester's name
(I knew him, Horatio; carnally;
a fellow of infinite yeast:
Uncle Toby!) with that of Yahoo
the publican, mine host to Marshal Stalk
and General Gloom, undercover characters
in Shag-spear the wordsmith.

Either way he lied, the clown,
or intuiting found employment
as coffin-maker, old mole
thundering in the earth.
He delved at Union speed, vertically;
with overtime, lied horizontally
at Union rates. No bonus there
for spading Denmark's royal sod,
rather a debit for the privilege.
Ophelia? Now that would be smelling.

I knew him, Horatio, pleaded the ponce,
namedropping *again*, sniffing around
for an imaginary friend and commonplace ego,
Horatio the skull, wally the first,
doublet, cod-piece and fireman's hose,
urgently translated into old Yorick,
toby and not toby, sans skulduggery.
Uncle this and uncle that.
Certainly the generation above.

The skull, Holbein's bonehead,
was (you guessed?) not Yorick's nor Yaughan's –
the worm i' the thighs embroiled –
but that of his da', old Hamlet,
the fellow in the cellarage,
quaffing the vintage, '37 and '38.
Otherwise, he wandered the battlements,
inebriated insomniac, superannuated extra,
deep throat on the road to Copenhagen
fortified with Tom Kyd's Spanish omelette
(chef's choice), tragedy with two veg.

Vomited, my friend, on the battlements; and swore:
the cock with fucking russet mantle combed.
Osric the elephant, Osric the antelope.
'Tis here! 'Tis here! 'Tis gone!

And Hamlet (young Hamlet) used wild and swirling words:
mazzard, loggits, quiddities, quillets,
statutes, recognizances, recoveries, vouchers –
what, for *another* lunch? Where had he been?
To the dictionary to compound confusion.

Ophelia. Remember Ophelia? he confided in his dad,
interested only in talking about Gertrude.
The actor cut his chin as he had a go –
I have a go, lady – at his three-day designer stubble.
Christ, he thought, she couldn't even have made it
in a nunnery. And the cock crew. Again.
Same old cock, somewhere. On the battlements.
On the third day. The battlements. Elsisnore.

ANTHONY THWAITE

A READING OF DOCTOR SAMUEL JOHNSON'S NOTES ON THE PLAYS: 1765

3.1.173

the fiery glow-worm's eyes

I know not how *Shakespeare,* who commonly derived
his knowledge of nature from his own observation,
happened to place the glow-worm's light in his
eyes, which is only in his tail.

The fiery glow-worm's eyes, the poisonous fork
That darts between the adder's lips, the stone
Encircling virtue in the old toad's brow,
Those bells of Bennet in Illyria . . .
How strangely careless of the antique Bard
To be so ignorant, confused, and quaint,
Lacking the advantages we possess –
We who see nature plain, who have no time
For superstition or bad geography,
Find Ariel trifling, and must smile to hear
Of rapiers two centuries too soon
Or how Morocco's Prince slew Persia's Sophy.
Indulgently we see him prattle on.
But he lived long ago, in simpler days.

PETER READING

POEM

Thick rhododendrons curtained the, even then,
mouldering disused outside proscenium,
crumbling dais backed by a stuccoed cowl
from which a player's lines would be ricocheted
into the bosky shades of a city park's
shrubby, neglected corner. A Lower IVth
strutted the wormed boards cockily *Out, outing,*
callowly slighting time and Melpomene.

Urinous, burnt-out, relic of civic wealth
29 years on: wintery sun projects
(onto flaked stucco daubed with despair-runes) a
palimpsest walking shadow. A fingernail
rot-tests the wreckage, strays to a middle-aged
wattle of jowl-flab, substance of candle-wax.

MICHAEL SCHMIDT

ALL.HAPPINESSE.AND.THAT.ETERNITIE.

One by one your friends
Fell to the force of sensible arrangements,
Sowed themselves in prosperous soil and grew
Their various houses. In the high windows
Children's faces showed, and they came down.
We aged, our taproots deep in compromise

And money. We have become a benign forest now,
A little jealous of your doubtful liberty.
We patronise you as we do the memory
Of our own youth, as though you were a child
Who touched in us a silted innocence.

Free spirit! Free within this loving forest
Where you are home a few more easy years –
If there were a room here large enough
It would be yours for ever, as we are.
But can you settle with those words that are
Air and your air, and on what countryscape
Whose shapes conceal the lover that you seek?

ROY FULLER

SHAKESPEARE STUDIES

1. Notes Towards a Shakespearean Sonnet

This sonnet puzzles all the critics, says
The Cambridge editor.
Should 'interim', 'winter', and 'today'
Simply be thought of as mere metaphors
Which love needs to recover from the lust
That's satisfied? Not poetry of knowledge,
But feelings, Ransom said (perhaps unjust).
And Samuel Butler, writing far from college,
Argued a buxom Royal Navy cook,
No noble sprig. Was Stratford to revise,
And rearrange, and make a printed book
(As Bridges wondered) – thwarted by his demise?
   The student looks up, sees a gold cascade
   Stuck to tweed shoulder-blades.

2. Exit Mistress Quickly

Flurries of white – but brought in on our shoes
They prove to be the palest lavender;
Unmelting, too, like the legendary snow
On Russki footwear of the First World War.

My feeble heart accentuates the chill
Of Spring. I'm struck how fitting the report is
Of Falstaff's death; and almost glad no hands
Explore the measure of my *rigor mortis*.

DANNIE ABSE

A CONSPICUOUS COUPLE

You and you are sure together
As the winter to foul weather.   As You Like It

Bubbles, brass, gaudy things, they loved well,
all that glitters and is starred,
the seven fairground colours swanking
on the bevelled edge of glass –
she, dramatic as a sunset,
he, chromatic like a rainbow
or an oilpool in the yard.

Love, agog, italic, rang their bell:
her computer flashing like a million,
he, randy, sighing like a villain;
she spread, he swooped, a kingfisher,
a kind of flying oilpool –
how they fluttered, how they fired,
till they guttered on her bed.

Naughty Aphrodite (minus nightie)
surely blessed them when they married,
outstaining the stained church window;
not the spermless priest who muttered,
'With this paintbox I thee wed,
a sunset to a rainbow
or an aurora borealis.'

The best man's innuendoes –
he was importune and loaded;
the aunts goofy and embarrassed
for no kiss could be more sexy
to erect in church a boudoir.
And big the triumph of the organ
when, promptly, the choirboys exploded.

PETE MORGAN

'GET THEE GLASS EYES:

And, like a scurvy politician, seem
To see things thou dost not.'   King Lear. Act IV, Scene VI

The politician and the poet
Share initial P's
Plus a little more despite
The poet's palinode of pleas
To contemplate the apposite
To be's, or not to be's.

To be the one P is to be
A grafter in the art
Of making language glorify
The humphing of the heart
With verbiage and verity –
If not in toto, then in part.

The P of polished platitudes
Will win acceptance late.
The youngster is the parvenu
Who waits his age. Negate
The image of a rise in ruse
From rat to reprobate.

Negate the notion of the P –
The upstarts; red or read –
Who knows the bubble of repute.
In this life, lately lead,
The living win dubiety.
The most revered? The dead!

To be the one P leering in
To P's glass eye might gloat
On that reflection of the self
Which is the truth. Connote
The mirror image might behind
The adverse opposition vote.

The poet and the politician
Wring the change in view
From the good eye to the bad –
From left to right. Between the two
Lies honesty, dishonesty.
The false reflects the true.

DAVID HARSENT

THE ANALYSAND

*I have had a dream, past the wit of man to say
what dream it was.*   A Midsummer Night's Dream

Just on the cusp of sleep
the image of a hare, hunkered
in the lee of a blackthorn hedge,

a sloping snowfield, a spinney,
the moon like a crooked sixpence ...
She'd expected to know the place.

It was dawn from the smell
of bacon in the pan
and the brisk riddling of coals.

She fetched him out, his boots
breaking the snowcrust
in Church Lane, the dogs at heel;

and, oh, he did it perfectly –
clapping against the cold
so that the sound

could reach her at one remove;
stopping to watch a heron;
lifting one hand, like someone

bowling under-arm,
to release the dogs. A rustle
of breath like silver-leaf

touched his lips as he started
to tackle the hill.
In that air, she could see

prisms in the spindrift
off his toecaps. No matter;
she was smug with speed.

As he stamped up
the steepest pitch, just past
the spinney and rose

towards her (so close
that she almost laughed)
she leapt into wakefulness.

*   *   *

I can't tell why,
but the most important part
was fetching him out:

his handclap coming at me
a pulse-beat late, the way
he set the dogs running.

I was lying-up
in the lee of a hedge; even so,
I could see everything

as if I sat on his shoulder;
and it came, remember,
on the cusp of sleep. –

Didn't you say
those are the truest dreams?
Well, I was puss,

a flibbertigibbet, familiar
to some wise old woman.
What do you make of it? Is he still

working the dogs on the down?
Will my children be harelipped
and my gaze mildew the grain?

JOHN COTTON

MATTHEW GOFFE

'And thither I will send you Matthew Goffe'
Lord Scales in 'Henry VI Part 2'
Act IV Scene V

Words uttered, like the thrown stone,
Cannot be called back.
They and their echoes haunt
The caves of dark theatres
Where they settle like dust
Waiting to be revived.
As Matthew Goffe waits
Faintly haunting his play.
You'll find him if you look
In the Dramatis Personae.
A name, like those on the memorial stones
Of the long abandoned dead,
Dispossessed and open
To the invention of characters,
Ready for development like vacant lots.
Hints are there: Matthew, bold, reliable,
A leader, he'd prop the citizens of Smithfield.
He is sent and dies in a brief wordlessness.
(Which is more than we know
Of the man who passes us in the street.)
It is as if Shakespeare was keeping him by
For a play that never came.
So he is available.
You need a character?
I will send you Matthew Goffe.

A. L. ROWSE

LINES FOR WILLIAM SHAKESPEARE

Reading in a book I came upon the words
In some dull prose, 'Thou hast nor youth nor age
But, as it were, an after-dinner's sleep
Dreaming on both.' The words leaped from the page:
Surprised, I suddenly found myself in tears.
There was that voice, the very rhythm and accent,
Simple, familiar, yet unmistakable,
Reaching across the yet unnumbered years,
The centuries, to touch the human heart.
And now again he says, 'There's no art
To find the mind's construction in the face.'
But in the magical mastery of phrase
That reaches the hidden crevices of guilt,
Remorse for what is irremediable,
That strips away pretence, hypocrisy,
The blindness to what we've done, and bares the wound.
One can hardly bear to look – a scene in a play
No longer, but the truth of life itself:
The bitter words of Hamlet to his love,
Because he loves, but believes he is betrayed;
Macbeth's wife, walking in her sleep,
Washing her hands, but blood will not away.
Leontes looks upon the ruin of his life,
Reconcilement, forgiveness at the last.
Lear to the daughter he had disowned,
'Your sisters have, as I do remember, done
Me wrong. You have some cause; they have not.'
To which Cordelia: 'No cause, no cause.'

'Put out the light, and then put out the light.'
'The odds is gone, and there is nothing left
Remarkable beneath the visiting moon.'
Such words sear the heart, and search the brain.
There never has been anyone like him,
Nor, come what may, will ever be again.

JOHN FULLER

DAUGHTER

"... ignorant of what thou art ...   The Tempest, I.ii

Once inside my head
The thought is hard to get out:
    Another daughter.

You were never ours.
Photographs showed you missing
    And no one noticed.

Intention was blind:
How near was your conception
    We shall never know.

The disqualified
Candidates can't believe the
    Office is unfilled.

You don't exist, but
Nobody can take your place:
    That space has been booked.

Three faces suggest
The fourth: compass points of the
    Parental axes.

Words like little loves
Presiding over a map
    For future journeys.

Prospero's secret
Sadness: I had peopled else
   This isle with daughters.

Only the subject
Of unuseful poetry:
   What never occurred.

ALAN BROWNJOHN

WAR-THOUGHTS

now that I have returned and that war-thoughts
Have left their places vacant, in their rooms
Come thronging soft and delicate desires . . .
        – Much Ado About Nothing

This is the day when our brave boys are safely returning.
The flowers and the bunting, which drape every street,
have been sponsored by Chambers of Commerce to fête
their homecoming, whose victory has rendered our pride
and rejoicing complete. Our boys, too, feel proud – of the
courage they showed for the nation with sheath-knives
and missiles. Their honour will not be put down. Their
honour is sacred, such honour has been our salvation.
The military virtues are back in town: our boys will have
fought with a far cleaner spirit than others, and not once
succumbed to strange vices in soft, scarlet rooms, in
foreign flop-houses frequented unknown to their
mothers. Our boys will have sent them back postcards of
classical tombs, and Renaissance chantries.

    Their war was our video game. Their privations were
set out in graphics that whirled on the screen, while
mandarins from Defence, with their charts and statistics,
were showing in detail the world that our boys would
have seen. When our boys turn the corner and enter the
square in procession, their feet will stamp once and be
still, the line come to a stop. The scaling of fifes and
bombardment of side-drums will lessen, our hearts miss
their beat as the rifle-butts drop with one crash to the
ground. They will stand up erect, no one falters, while
wreaths of respect are laid over the previous dead; and

then march off again, to break up and disperse to their quarters, where some of our boys will crawl gratefully off to their bed.

But others will flourish their swords in the thirsty environs of bar and casino and dance-hall, and shout battle-songs; at bus-stops at midnight will curse – and be cursed by – civilians not proud of our boys for redressing their wrongs. Their officers, though, will lie stretched out in exquisite arbours, enhancing their peace with anthologies of trees; and to-night will assume elaborate helmets – for dancing; and go in for drawing up battlefield strategies – of love; and each delicate move of love's quarries will show on their sigint computers precisely. Thus, turning up for the Governor's Reception, one young blood, the bravest, will know where to find the best beauty and come at the spoils of his war.

ROGER WODDIS

LEARNING FROM THE MASTER

I dreamt that I was supping with the Bard;
The hour was late and we had drunk our fill.
I said, 'To write a poem's bloody hard –
But not for you. How do you do it, Will?'

He drained his pewter jug and rubbed his beard,
Then said, 'God's wounds, it helps to be insane:
I think of all I've lost and loved and feared,
And day by day carve slices off my brain.'

'But wait,' I countered, 'what about the Muse?
If inspiration doesn't play a part,
Do you rely on quantities of booze
To body forth the secrets of the heart?'

He shook his head at my naïve suggestion:
'Sometimes it flows, sometimes I slave all night.
"To be, or not to be: that is the question" –
That took all week before I got it right.

'But though there is no substitute for sweat,
Immortal lines expressing what is true
Can happen when you're at the launderette,
Boiling an egg or sitting in the loo.'

D. J. ENRIGHT

NEW READINGS

Goneril
Think of what she had to put up with.
The old fellow complaining of the food,
Bringing his drunken cronies home,
A hundred of them!
Interfering with the domestics,
Breaking the china.
Such language too!
She wasn't a saint.

Regan
The house was too small.
She was out of provisions.
She had to keep up with the Albanys.
So down with the cronies –
From fifty to twenty-five to none at all.
She wasn't a miracle worker.

Angelo
Anybody can get hooked on a nun.
Especially a monk. He knew he'd done wrong,
Or tried to.
Up till then he was quite sincere.
And he did marry Mariana.

Octavius
A trifle severe? But he had a job to do.
Not all of us can spare the time
To fool around with foreign females.
And look at the way his sister was treated.
Yet he composed a nice obituary for Antony,
He said his death should make a bigger noise.
That was big of him.

Coriolanus
An officer and a gentleman.
It was the politicians brought him down.
Pity he married that mousy girl.
'O! no, no, no' was all she could say.
A mother isn't the same thing.

Lady Macbeth
A good wife advances her husband's career.
She poured out spirits for him
And told him to wash his hands.
He didn't really appreciate her.

Caliban
They taught him language, and
Most of it was bad.
Perhaps the British Council was mistaken,
And they ought to have taught him literature?
But that would have been wrong too.

Hamlet
He was less than kind.
If it hadn't been for him
Ophelia would have married a Gentleman
And had babies,
Polonius died in bed, incontinent but content,
Those good chums Rosencrantz and Guildenstern
Pursued philosophy and fräuleins in the taverns,
While Claudius took the government in hand
And perhaps a youthful mistress.
The villain of the piece is plain to see,
His name is hidden in the title.

PENELOPE SHUTTLE

THE HORSE WHO LOVES ME

King Richard: "A horse! a horse! my kingdom for a horse!"
Richard III, Act V Scene IV

1.
The horse who loves me is strong and unsaddled.
He desires to learn nothing.
He sleeps standing, like a tree.
He lifts dawn on his willing shoulders.

I ride the horse who loves me,
hands twined in his bashful mane,
knees gripping his nut-butter flanks.

The horse who loves me goes on tiptoe,
his hooves tap the fiery earth.
The long leisure of his muzzle pleases me.

His smell is salt and primroses, honeycomb
and furnace. Oh the sweat of his glittering tail!
How he prances studiously, the horse who loves me.

The horse who loves me has no hobby but patience.
He brings me the gift of his honesty.
His big heart beats with love.
Sometimes he openly seeks a wife. But he returns to me.

The horse who loves me is one of the poor of Paradise.
He enjoys Paradise as such a loving horse might,
quietly watching the seven wonders of the night.

2.
Look at my horse!
His neatly-plaited snowy tail
hands like a fine finger between his pearly buttocks.
His name can be Desire, or Brother.

He does not complain of my weight on his back
any more than darkness complains of its loneliness.

The horse who loves me
wields the prick of pain that caps the dart of love.
We gasp at its pang,
then race for the scaled wall of the sky.

The horse who loves me
takes me beyond the lengths grief goes to,
beyond the strides joy makes,
beyond the moon and his sister the future.

This heaven-kissing horse of mine
takes me with him to his aerial home.
Below us, roofs grey, fields fade, rivers shiver, pardoned.
I am never coming back.

DAVID SWEETMAN

FORTUNE AND MEN'S EYES

In the blood, unseen
and unforgiving,
when tears are lenses that magnify
the shifting continents of pain.

The world ends slowly as it began,
each day a peak added to the mountains,
each night the body's comforting return
to that first solitary embrace.

So much is aluminium,
the dead colour of our century,
bowls and pans with nervous sideways glances,
the familiar, accusing El Greco on a tap.

How pleasantly nature lies:
the flush of ripeness, the fascinating bruise.
A hand plucks a modest valentine
and squeezes out its dimpled heart,

grapes jangle severed nerves,
their pips neatly ordered on a plate.
Count them: he loves me, she loves me not,
she loves me, he loves me not . . .

You may force out any answer that you wish
and taste how bittersweet fingers are,
a mere tissue's width from the vengeful flow
at war with love.

EDWIN MORGAN

THE BEAR

Come here, come here, I'm really playful today,
don't be afraid, they've even made me a chair
or a hammock of sorts I love to loll in
and surprise my visitors. I am never hungry
since I took this part. No no, I don't mean him,
Antigonus. Good lord, as soon as we're off stage
we jink a little sweet rough tumble together
as like a dance as you ever saw, nothing
like death, nothing like death. I like that man.
He gives me herring from the brown barrel.
He gives me beer and honey once a week.
I could tear the lid right off that barrel
with a swipe and stuff myself stiff with fish
but I don't. I nuzzle the man. I get enough.
The only one I can't like is that Perdita,
she's a hussy in all that greenery-yallery,
with her pert stamping foot, his I should say,
these boys are a saucy pampered lot,
if they got some women I would really dance.
Antigonus though, he seems to like bears.
Strange man, but good. He won't change.
I love to creep up on him, hardly
breathing, stand at his back and tap
his shoulder. He never jumps,
just smiles. 'This is the chase,'
he says, 'we must go on for ever.'

GAVIN EWART

THE ORACLE SPEAKS IN THE DRESSING ROOM OF MR. PATRICK STEWART AT THE BARBICAN, BEFORE A PERFORMANCE OF *THE WINTER'S TALE*

The blood shall flood erectile tissue
and Lost and Found shall be the issue.
True woman, screeching like a mynah,
truth shall be spoken by Paulina.
Courtiers shall dine on rich and rare food,
Antigonus shall end as bearfood.
Mamillius shall die, mum-missing,
too young for court or country kissing.
Unwanted characters, however spot on,
shall be knocked out to help the plot on.
Dramatic irony and fitness!
A whole ship's crew goes – there's no witness!

Autolycus, no Montezuma,
shall give the thing a dash of humour,
and Love shall grow, by Chance much pandered –
for what's unlikely here is standard.
Coincidence shall stare straight at you,
the King believe his wife's a statue;
sensitive as an armadillo,
shall give Paulina to Camillo!
All shall end well, all shall be friends here,
Apollo won't allow loose ends here,
Genius shall win (Will has his way)
but it's a pretty funny play!

LAURENCE COTTERELL

DEEPMAN CAIUS KENT

With Kent, Will's fooled us long enough –
    Lear's Earl of Kent, the "true-blue Englishman"
    To every critic of that god-strewn play.

What a dissembler in the guise of Caius,
    And what a stirrer even in the stocks,
    To get Lear roaring leonine anew!

It took the villain Cornwall to detect
    The subtlety beneath the coarse cloak of abuse:
    The mask "a saucy roughness", rudely shown.
(Yet still "the very man"
    That from Lear's "first of difference and decay"
    Played on the diplomat and saved the realm,
    Clad in the garb and bearing of a churl.)

And who but Kent pierced through
    The jester's motley shield
    To find philosopher in cap and bells? –
The deepman Kent, not only oath and sword:
    "This is not altogether fool, my lord."

PATRICIA BEER

NINNY'S TOMB

I'll meet thee, Pyramus, at Ninny's tomb.
Ninny, you may have laughed in the wrong place
But you are not a noisy spirit. Now
You are as airless as your crop of grass.

It is a quiet night. The sea has lost
Its voice, though it lies plump and blooming
Beyond the monumental arch through which
They brought you in to your dead-serious homing.

You are the founding father of wantwits,
Thesaurus silly-billy, noodle, loon.
Not verb or adjective. You cannot do
Or qualify. You are a proper noun.

Pyramus, Thisbe, Moonshine and the Lion
Come here, and so do I and many another
Whom certainly the good Duke will not ask
To roar again. Ninny, our clone, our brother.

I think you clowned your way into your coffin,
Your feet up where your shoulders ought to go,
Or turned on to your face to get a laugh.
Ninny, please do not ask me how I know.

PETER REDGROVE

SISTER
(Mudlark XX)

Sister of the wet wings
Of your gown, misty Ophelia,
You have survived
The electricity of your insanity,
It flows down the stream harmlessly,
Your stench of love not retuned,
Replaced with water's clean oozy ozone;

Thoroughly doused,
Smelling of clean mud,
Immaculate mud,
Sinless beady ooze and waterweed,
These perfumes
Scenting your bedroom,
Watery sister, you return.

Calm as the flower
Drenched in this thunderstorm
You offer me the nenuphar to smell,
You offer me the water-lily
Rooted in mud to smell,
Its spirit mingles
With the river-perfume of your chest,
The potion pouring off your throat which is bare
In wings of invisibility
On which a new regime soars,
And unarmoured ghosts
With puffed sleeves and open throats
Roam the corridors of Elsinore;

You have come into the succession at last;
It crackles around you in a new
White satin blouse which is queenly and mad.

CHARLES TOMLINSON

VARIATION

And there is nothing left remarkable
Beneath the visiting moon.

-Antony and Cleopatra, 4. vii

What is left remarkable beneath the visiting moon
  Is the way the horizon discovers itself to be
The frontier of a country unseen till this:
  Soon the light will focus the whole of it
Under one steadying beam, but now in rising
  Still has to clear the brow of a hill
To unroll the unmapped differences here,
  Where the floor of the valley refuses to appear
Uncoped by the shadow of its flank: it is the speed
  That accompanies this deed of climbing and revealing
Marks the ascent: you can measure out the pace
  Of the unpausing visitant between tree and tree,
Setting each trunk alight, then hurrying on
  To shine back down over the entire wood
It has ignited to flicker in white. Free
  From the obstructions it has come burning through
It has the whole of the night sky to review
  The world below it, seeming to slow
And even to dream its way. It does not arrive alone
  But carries the memory of that spread of space
And of the aeons across which it has shone till now
  From the beginning. This is the illumination it pours
Into the shadows and the watcher's mind,
  As it touches on planes of roofs it could not foresee
Shaping and sharing its light when it set out
  In a rain of disintegrating comets, of space creating.